GEOGRAPHY OF THE AMERICAS

Contents

MW00824000

This is how Earth looks from space. The two continents shown here are North America and South America.

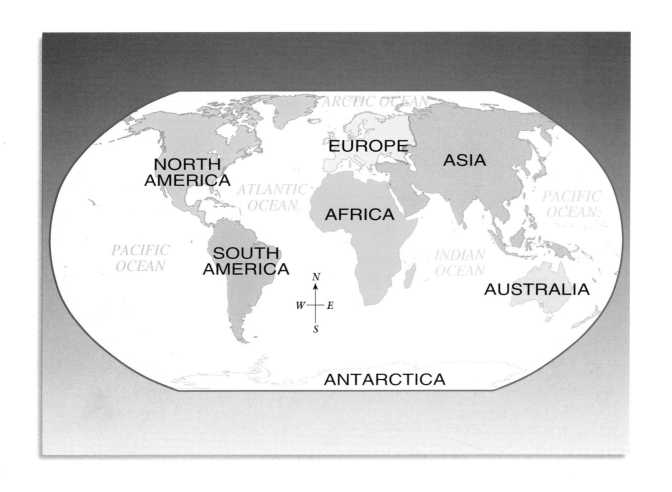

This is a map of the world. There are
seven continents and four oceans.

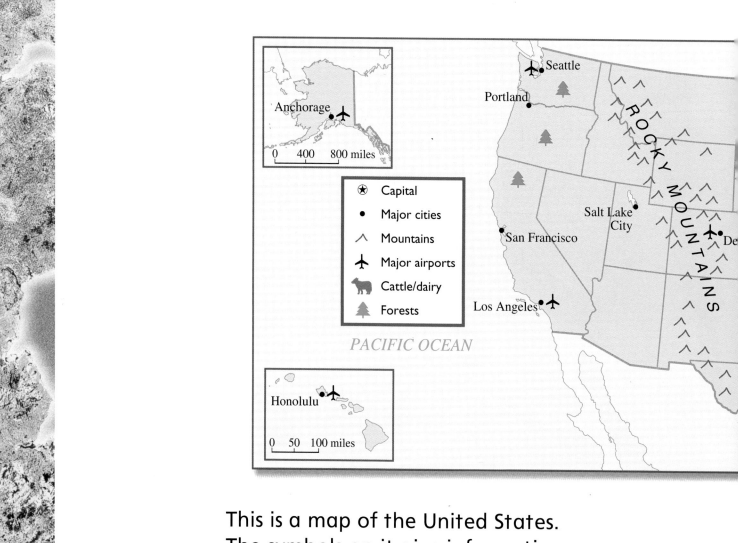

Legend

- ⊛ Capital
- • Major cities
- ⋀ Mountains
- ✈ Major airports
- 🐑 Cattle/dairy
- 🌲 Forests

This is a map of the United States.
The symbols on it give information.

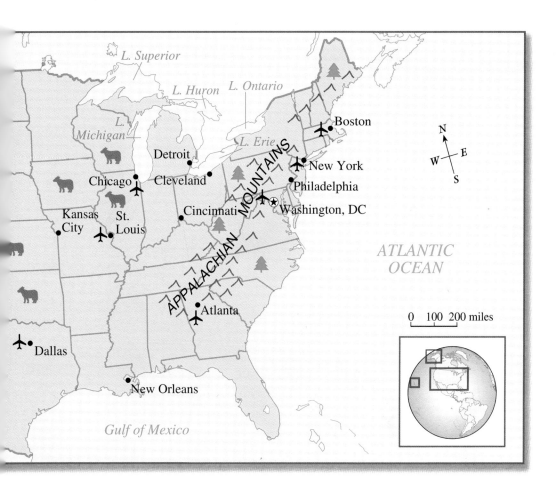

What symbol is used to show Washington, D.C.?
Why is it different from the other symbol for cities?

Products are shipped on the Mississippi River. Many places like St. Louis were started along the river and grew into big cities.

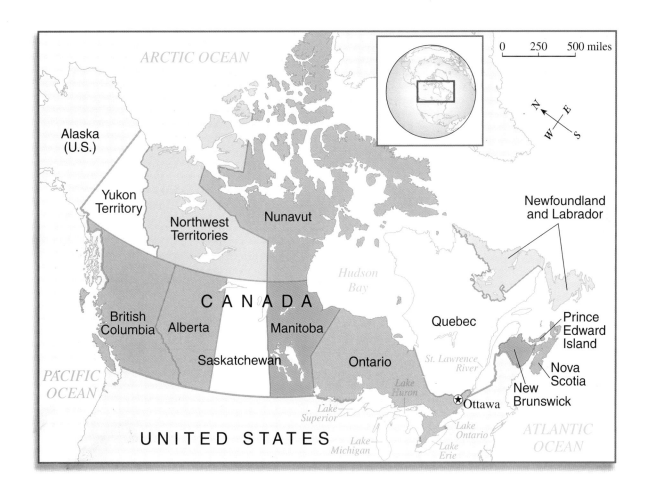

Canada is a very large country.
It is our neighbor to the north.

The maple leaf is part of the Canadian flag.
The British queen is shown on Canadian money.

8

Long ago, the Aztec Empire ruled Mexico. This painting shows people working in the great city of the Aztecs.

This is a factory in Mexico today. Workers peel apples and put them on a moving belt. The apples will be made into applesauce.

This map shows the seven countries of
Central America. They are south of Mexico.

The West Indies is made up of many islands.
Some are large. Others are quite small.

There are three flags on the building in this picture. The flag of Puerto Rico is between the flags of the United States and Spain.

This map shows the countries of South America.

São Paulo is a city in Brazil. There are tall buildings and lots of traffic. Many people live in São Paulo.

Rain forests are important. Many special plants and animals like this spotted frog live in the rain forests.

Simón Bolívar wanted the Spanish colonies in South America to be independent countries. He led the fight for independence.

Quito is the capital of Ecuador.
It is high in the Andes Mountains.

The Incas built Machu Picchu a long time ago.
It was not easy to build a city so high in the
mountains.

A long time ago, people traveled on Lake Titicaca in boats like this. Today, most people use motorboats like those in the background.

This map shows the part of South America called the Southern Cone. There are four countries there.

There are huge cattle ranches in Argentina.
They are on grassland called the pampas.
The cowboys are called gauchos.

José de San Martín fought for independence in South America. He is shown on the left.

Eva Perón cared about the people in Argentina. They cared about her, too. These young soccer players are glad to meet her.